Examination
of
Consience

for
Children
Ages 6 to 12

CHARLES MICHAEL

Gifted Books and Media

Copyright

Compiled by Charles Michael

Printed in the United States of America

Published in February 2020

Paperback ISBN: 978-1-947343-07-8

Published by Jayclad Publishing LLC
www.giftedbookstore.com

Table of Contents

Note to Parents

- This book is suitable for kids, six years old up to twelve years old

- The book can be introduced in small portions for younger kids

- Some of the areas mentioned can be implemented within the home without the need for going to confession

- This book acts as not only a guide to confession but a tool to instill good Christian values in a child

- This book is not meant to replace or substitute the formal CCD/ CCE/ Sunday classes/ Catechism that a child will have to enroll in to learn about the Catholic faith

- Parental supervision is a must for kids which holds true also when studying this book

- It is the parent's responsibility to take the child for confession regularly

- The parents have to foremost build and maintain a Christian atmosphere at home by praying together and going to church regularly, which in turn will bring godliness in the child

Note to the Child

- This book is a tool to examine your conscience to prepare for a good confession

- Not everything mentioned in this book is to be taken as a mortal sin or even requires confession

- This book is a tool that will help you become a good Christian and help you to identify areas that prevent you from going closer to God

- It is a good practice to make notes while reading this book

Do's and Don't's of Confession

- Do not give any excuse (justify) for your sins

- Do not blame people or circumstances for your sins

- Be truly sorry for your sins when you confess

- Do not be too detailed when you are confessing your sins

- When you confess a sin, also mention the number of times you committed that sin

- Do not leave out any sin

- Do not postpone your confession

- Confess your sins regularly, if possible, weekly

- Do not be afraid about confessing to a priest. Go to any available priest

- Do not receive communion in a state of mortal sin. Confess your mortal sins before receiving communion

- Be sure to get rid of everything that tempts or leads you to sin

- Confess only your sins, not your problems

- Do not confess the sins of others

- Be mindful of the priest's time and others in line

- If in doubt about the seriousness of a sin, confess to the priest

- Do not feel bad or ashamed to confess any sin

- Do not hide your sins

- Do not lie in the confessional

- Do not make a false and insincere confession

- Do not make up sins just because you were told to go for confession

- Do not confess a sin if it was already confessed and not committed

- Daily examination of conscience is better and effective than trying to come up with a sin in the last minute to confess

- Confessing venial sins helps us to be more sensitive to God and be more faithful in our love to Him

- It is a good practice to write down our sins and take it to confession

- For a sin to be mortal, three conditions must be met: Mortal sins are sins that are grave (serious) in matter and that which is also committed with full knowledge and free will (full consent)

- Make reparation and restitution where and when necessary (If you have stolen something, return it)

- Forgive everyone with all your heart (unconditionally) so that God may also forgive you

- Pray to the Holy Spirit to show you all hidden sins and to be filled with a heart of repentance

- Do not fail to do the penance given by the priest

- Be thankful for God's forgiveness

The Ten Commandments

List of the Ten Commandments

- I am the Lord your God. You shall have no other gods before me

- You shall not make wrongful use of the name of the Lord your God

- Remember to keep the sabbath day holy

- Honor your father and your mother

- You shall not kill

- You shall not commit adultery

- You shall not steal

- You shall not bear false witness against your neighbor

- You shall not covet your neighbor's wife

- You shall not covet your neighbor's goods

Where in the Bible, do we find the Ten Commandments?

The Ten Commandments are listed in two places in the Old Testament. It is listed in Exodus, chapter 20, and Deuteronomy, chapter 5.

How are the Ten Commandments divided?

The first three commandments speak about our relationship with God. The remaining seven speak about our relationship with our neighbor.

Who gave the Ten Commandments?

The Ten Commandments were written by God on two stone tablets and given to Moses on Mount Sinai.

What is the greatest commandment?

Love is the greatest and the only commandment.

The First Commandment

*I am the LORD, your God. You shall have no other
gods before me*

My Relationship with God

- Do I see God as my Father?

- Do I see God as someone who always loves me?

- Do I see God as someone who cares for me?

- Do I see God as someone who wants to help me?

- Do I see God as merciful and forgiving?

- Do I see God as all-powerful and good?

- Do I see Jesus as my friend and brother?

- Do I see the Holy Spirit as my helper and guide?

Prayer

- Do I pray every day?

- Do I begin each day in prayer?

- Do I pray each night before going to bed?

- Have I forgotten to say my morning and evening prayers?

- Have I deliberately not prayed because of sleepiness or tiredness?

- Do I seal myself with the Sign of the Cross daily and regularly?

- Do I share everything with God?

- Do I maintain proper posture when I pray?

- Have I been moody and rebellious about prayer?

- Do I see prayer as boring and unexciting (tiring)?

- Am I always told or forced to pray by my family members?

- Do I complain about prayer?

- Do I show tiredness and sleepiness when I pray?

Know God (Reading about God)

- Do I read the Bible daily to know about God?

- Do I pray to the Holy Spirit for wisdom and understanding to help me with knowledge about God?

- Do I read about saints to know their love for God?

- Do I have a children's version of the catechism (Youcat for Kids) and read it regularly?

- Have I memorized all the basic Catholic prayers?

- Do I show interest in watching good Christian and Catholic movies?

- Do I watch Good Christian movies to grow in the knowledge of God?

- Do I take an interest in knowing about the various Christian holidays (feasts) and their meanings?

Holy Bible

- Do I have my own children's Bible?

- Do I read the Bible daily and regularly?

- Do I familiarize myself with the various books of the Bible?

- Do I share the Bible stories with others and talk about it at home and outside?

- Do I cherish the Bible and not treat it like any other book?

Mother Mary, Saints, and Angels

- Do I pray to Mother Mary every day for her help and intercession?

- Do I pray the Rosary every day?

- Do I seek the help of my Guardian Angel every day for protection?

- Do I pray to my patron saint for his or her intercession?

Idol Worship

- Have I made an idol of sportspersons, superheroes, or entertainment figures (movie stars and pop stars), therefore forgetting the importance of God?

- Have I given more importance to anything (toys, gadgets, friends, fun) other than God?

- Do I fantasize or desire to have any supernatural quality or gift inspired and influenced by the movies and shows I watch?

- Do I value my toys to be more important than God?

- Do I see Christian holidays (Christmas, Easter) as a time, only to receive gifts, wear new clothes, and eat candy?

Occult (Evil)

- Have I read any occult novels or literature (Harry Potter, Twilight Series, Etc.)?

- Do I have any occult novels or books at home?

- Have I used Ouija boards or tarot cards as a toy?

- Have I watched any occult (evil) television shows or movies?

- Do I have an interest in horror movies or shows?

- Have I willingly watched horror movies and shows?

Superstition

- Do I believe in lucky numbers?

- Do I believe in lucky colors?

- Do I believe in superheroes, fairies, and other unreal creatures?

- Do I believe in luck?

- Do I believe in objects to bring me good luck?

- Do I follow practices that are said to bring good luck?

- Do I give more importance to any traditions or practices other than Jesus during Christmas?

Confession (Sacrament of Reconciliation)

- Am I regular to confession?

- Have I lied in the confessional?

- Have I failed, or did I ever forget to do the penance given by the priest?

- Have I hidden any sins in a confession (insincere confession)?

- Did I confess without being truly sorry for the sin?

- Have I shown a lack of interest in going for confession?

- Did I make up any sin because I was told to go for confession ?

- Did I get impatient when standing in line for confession?

- Did I willingly overhear anybody's confession?

- Did I confess without being sorry for my sins?

The Second Commandment

You shall not take the name of the Lord your God in vain

Use of God's Name

- Have I used God's name carelessly?

- Have I used God's name irreverently (without respect)?

- Do I use God's name in anger?

- Have I used God's name in any casual joke?

- Have I cursed using God's name?

- Have I laughed or shown interest when somebody shared a joke that spoke about God in a bad way or made fun of God?

- Have I continued to watch a movie that spoke about God in the wrong way?

- Do I read or have books that speak about God in a bad way?

- Did I ever get angry at God?

Be Thankful

- Am I thankful for the gift of life?

- Am I thankful for my Catholic faith?

- Am I thankful for my parents?

- Am I thankful for my siblings?

- Am I thankful for all my grandparents?

- Am I thankful for my home?

- Am I thankful for the finances (money) that my parents have?

- Am I thankful that my parents have a job?

- Am I thankful for my body, the way it is?

- Do I complain about my weaknesses and failures?

- Am I thankful for the daily food?

- Am I thankful for my school and education?

- Am I thankful for my grades?

- Am I thankful for my teachers and their dedication?

- Am I thankful for all my cousins and relatives?

- Am I thankful for all my friends?

- Do I complain about the lack of toys?

- Do I compare what I have to what other children have and feel unhappy about it?

- Am I thankful for my good health?

- Am I thankful for my gifts and talents?

- Do I complain about the lack of comforts at home?

- Am I able to see myself as blessed?

Church

- Do I genuflect when I enter and exit the church (sanctuary)?

- Do I bless myself with holy water when I enter and exit the church?

- Do I disturb my parents when they are praying in the church?

- Do I maintain total silence in church when I am asked to?

- Do I use (play with) my phone or gadget in church?

- Do I bring toys to Church and play with them during Mass or prayer service?

Holy Objects

- Do I treat blessed objects such as the Rosary, scapulars, Holy Bible, blessed images, holy water, and the Crucifix with respect and care?

- Have I played with or used any holy (blessed) object as a toy?

- Do I keep some kind of blessed object for protection at all times?

Holy People

- Do I greet holy people such as priests, deacons, and nuns when I meet them?

- Do I pray for my parish priest?

- Have I made fun of any priest, nun, or other religious persons?

Promises

- Do I make promises and don't keep them?

- Did I use God's name when making promises to others?

The Third Commandment

Remember to keep the sabbath day holy

Lord's Day (Sunday)

- Do I spend Sundays solely on fun and entertainment?

- Do I sleep late, and am I reluctant to get out of bed on time on Sundays?

- Do I see Sunday as a day to watch television or to be on gadgets all day?

- Do I see Sunday as a day to play and be with my friends all day?

Holy Mass on Sundays

- Did I deliberately miss Mass on Sunday?

- Did my behavior/attitude make it difficult for my parents to get to church on time?

- Have I been moody and rebellious about going to church (Holy Mass) on Sundays?

- Am I distracted at Holy Mass?

- Do I join in the singing by using the hymn book?

- Do I attentively listen to the priest's homily?

- Do I look at the altar and not look at the people around me, while the Mass is going on?

- Do I disturb my parents during Holy Mass?

- Do I pay attention to the readings during the Mass?

- Do I respond to all the prayers during the Mass?

- Do I receive communion with reverence and love for Jesus?

- Do I engage in doing anything other than taking part in the Mass?

- Do I use my phone during the Mass?

- Have I memorized all the Mass prayers and joined others in reciting them?

- Did I play video games during the Mass?

- Did I text during the Mass?

- Am I tempted to look at my phone during the Mass?

- Do I daydream during Holy Mass?

- Do I dress well for Holy Mass?

- Have I gotten impatient during the Mass?

- Do I join with others in standing, kneeling, and offering peace during the Mass?

Daily Mass

- Do I go for daily Mass during school holidays (summer and winter break) if my parents are available to take me to church?

Holy Days of Obligation

- Am I aware that I should attend Mass on all holy days of obligation if my parents are available to take me to church?

Obedience to the Church

- Do I recite the Way of the Cross during Lent with my family or by myself?

- Do I make at least one sacrifice during lent and advent (giving up a cellphone, eating candy, watching television, etc.)?

Religious Education

- Have I shown a lack of interest in attending religious classes?

- Do I pay attention to all that is taught about God in Sunday classes?

- Did I show a lack of interest in learning about God?

- Do I sincerely prepare and have a desire to receive the Sacrament of Reconciliation and the First Holy Communion?

The Fourth Commandment

Honor your father and your mother

Love your Parents

- Do I allow my parents to spend time with one another?

- Have I ever grieved my parents?

- Do I understand the sacrifices my parents make for me and am I appreciative of them?

- Do I know the financial condition of my parents, and do I demand for things that my parents cannot afford?

- Do I understand the financial condition of my parents and not trouble them for more than what they can afford?

- Do I know and appreciate the hard work that my parents put in to run the family and raise me?

- Am I too demanding of my parents' time and attention that it hinders their work and responsibility?

- Am I too demanding of my parents' time and attention, especially when they come back from work and very tired?

- Have I ever taken sides when my parents fought?

- Do I spend time with my parents at home and not give all of my time to toys and gadgets (phone and tablet)?

- Do I help my parents?

- Do I always want to be with my friends?

- Do I love and treat both parents equally?

- Did I ever fight with my parents and not talk to them?

- Did I cause a fight or misunderstanding between my parents?

Honor your Parents

- Have I brought dishonor to my parents through my actions in school or outside of home?

- Have I made fun of my parents?

- Have I spoken against my parents to others?

- Have I ever been ashamed or embarrassed of my parents?

- Did I misbehave with my parents in public?

- Have I raised my voice (talk loud) to my parents?

- Have I spoken against my parents behind their backs?

- Do I share family secrets with friends?

- Have I spoken in a demanding way with my parents and elders?

- Have I ever physically hurt my parents?

- Have I ever said something to hurt my parents?

- Have I shown anger or hatred towards my parents?

Obey your Parents

- Do I always have to be rewarded for doing anything?

- Have I ever disobeyed my parents?

- Have I ever ignored the commands, warnings, or directions of my parents?

- Have I thrown tantrums to get my way?

- Do I whine when I am told to do something?

- Do I have to be repeatedly reminded or told to do things that are expected of me?

- Do I manipulate my parents with my tantrums?

- Do I deliberately do or say things that will cause my parents to lose their temper?

- Do I talk back to my parents, teachers, or elders?

- Have I shown disrespect to elders?

- Did I feel unloved at home when I was scolded for a mistake I did?

- Do I see discipline as something that goes against my freedom?

- Do I rebel against elders in the family?

- Did I act stubbornly in a store about getting a toy?

- Do I stay close to my parents when I am in a public place without straying away?

- Do I resort to crying to draw my parents' attention?

- Do I demand for things I need and act stubborn till I get it?

- Did I do anything against my parents' wishes?

Family Prayer

- Do I pray with my family every day?

- Do I pray for my parents every day?

- Do I pray for my siblings every day?

- Do I begin everything with a prayer?

- Do I pray for wisdom and knowledge in studies/academics?

- Do I pray for protection every day?

- Do I, in faith, lift the needs of the family in prayer?

- Do I cooperate when my parents ask me to pray?

- Do I pray for all my deceased (dead) family members?

- Do I pray for all my friends?

- Do I pray for all my relatives (grandparents, uncles, aunts, cousins, etc.)?

- Do I pray for my teachers?

- Do I pray for the leaders of the country?

- Do I say grace before meals?

- Do we pray the Rosary as a family?

- Do I pray before tests and exams?

Sibling Love

- Have I seen my sibling as a competitor?

- Have I seen my sibling as a rival?

- Do I act unkindly toward my siblings and fail to love them?

- Do I have trouble sharing things with my siblings?

- Do I fail to pray for my sibling?

- Do I get these thoughts that my parents love my sibling more than they like me?

- Do I feel that my parents give more time and attention to my siblings than to me?

- Do I get jealous and want my parents to pay attention only to me?

- Do I dominate my sibling in any way?

- Do I share my toys/stationery with my sibling?

- Have I started fights with my siblings or provoked them to anger?

- Have I spoken evil about my sibling to my parents or others?

- Do I always pick a fight with my sibling?

- Am I kind and gentle with my younger sibling?

- Do I give respect to my older sibling?

- Do I willingly include my sibling in play and games if they are around the same age as me?

Freedom

- Have I misused my freedom in any way?

- Do I complain about a lack of freedom at home?

- Do I watch anything on television or the internet without my parent's knowledge and permission?

- Have I misused the internet access that was given to me for things other than educational purposes and games approved by my parents?

- Did I purposely exceed the time I was given to use the internet or other media (gadgets)?

- Have I purchased or downloaded anything over the computer or phone without my parent's knowledge?

Sharing and Openness

- Do I share everything with my parents that is communicated to me by my teachers at school?

- Do I share with my parents about all the upcoming tests and homework that needs to be done?

- Have I hidden any bad grades that I scored or done something bad at school?

- Do I have any friends that my parents are not aware of?

- Do I have any sinful habit or addiction that my parents are not aware of?

- Do I have any sickness or pain that my parents are not aware of?

- Am I talking to or texting anyone that my parents are not aware of?

- Did I talk to any adult without my parent's knowledge either on the internet or in person?

- Is there any incident in my life (e.g., sexual abuse) that I am hiding from my parents?

- Do I make my parents part of everything in my life?

- Am I hiding any grave sin, habit, or wrongdoing from my parents?

- Have I lied to my parents about anything?

Honor Your Teachers

- Do I pay attention to all the instructions in class?

- Do I hand in all homework on time?

- Do I have to be repeatedly told to be focused in class?

- Have I misbehaved in school?

- Do I obey all school rules and class rules?

Education & Learning

- Do I show love and interest for learning?

- Do I watch too much television or browse the internet that hinders my education?

- Do I put my heart and best effort (hard work) in education and learning, or do I see it as a burden?

- Am I prompt in doing all my schoolwork on time?

- Do I deliberately make excuses to stay away from school and learning?

- Do I prepare well for tests and exams?

- Do I prepare well in advance for all my tests and exams and not try to study everything in one night (cramming)?

- Do I complain about education and homework?

- Do I show a lack of interest in education?

- Do I fail to seek God's help every day for my education?

- Do I pray to the Holy Spirit to help me understand what I learn and to remind me during tests and exams?

- Do I give more importance to games, sports, and entertainment than education?

- Do I see the value of education and learning and put my best effort into it?

- Do I go to school without being forced?

- Do my parents have to battle with me each morning to make me get out of bed and go to school?

- Do I make careless mistakes in my assignments because of my lack of attention and focus?

- Do I see education as my priority, and do I take the initiative to learn?

- Do I put extra time and effort into concepts (subjects) that I don't understand?

Household Chores and Cleanliness

- Do I have to be continuously told to do my daily chores and duties?

- Do I complain and resist to help my parents with household chores?

- Do I always have to be told to clean my room?

- Do I ignore my parents when I am told to do my chores?

- Does somebody always have to clean up after me?

- Do I have to be told repeatedly to do things around the house?

- Do I always leave the place messy after I work?

- Do I procrastinate (postpone doing my work)?

- Do I deliberately dirty the house?

- Do I keep my room clean?

- Do I take good care of my belongings (books and clothes)?

Taking Responsibility

- Do I take responsibility for everything I do?

- Do I go to bed on time on school nights?

- Do I wake up when I am asked to or when the alarm rings?

- Do I take responsibility for my schoolwork without being told or reminded?

- Do I lose my things frequently, or do things break easily because I don't pay attention?

Sharing

- Do I share my toys, gadgets, and stationery with my siblings and friends?

- Am I selfish?

- Does it make me sad when I have to share things with others?

The Fifth Commandment

You shall not Kill

Anger and Violence

- Have I ever resorted to violence to get my way?

- Do I have a liking for movies/shows with violence?

- Have I watched movies with excessive violence?

- Did I ever play overly rough in games?

- Have I gotten angry at anybody, or have I hit anyone?

- Have I destroyed any personal property, things at home, or school property as a result of my anger and temper?

- Do I get angry or restless when I get a "NO" from my parents?

- Do I easily get impatient?

Video games and Gaming Apps

- Have I played or downloaded video games or apps that are not suitable for my age?

- Have I played video games that promote violence and evil (shooting and killing)?

- Have I played video games that promote unchristian values?

- Have I played any video games that made me do something evil?

- Do I play video games that require me to do harmful things?

- Have I played video games that have some horror elements in them?

Television, Internet & Media

- Do I spend all my weekends watching television or browsing the internet?

- Have I watched anything on television (or the internet) without my parent's knowledge and consent?

- Do I promptly inform my parents if something inappropriate (unsuitable for my age) appears on the screen?

- Do I stay up late with my gadget without my parent's knowledge?

- Do I get angry and irritated if I am not allowed to watch television or browse the internet?

- Do I watch too much television, which hinders my family time and study time?

Smartphone / Tablet addiction

- Am I always on my phone?

- Do I complain when my gadget (smartphone, tablet) is taken away from me?

- Do I get irritated when my phone/gadget doesn't work because of low battery or no wifi (signs of addiction and dependence)

Texting

- Am I constantly texting my friends?

- Do I text while studying or eating?

- Do I text while walking or crossing the road?

- Do I text or receive texts outside of normal hours (late night)?

Chatrooms & Social Media

- Did I talk to any strangers (adults) in chatrooms or social media apps?

- Am I using any chat apps or social media apps and websites without my parents' knowledge or permission?

- Am I giving out any personal information to strangers without my parents' consent?

- Do I use any social media app beyond a reasonable amount of usage?

- Do my parents know all my social media friends?

- Do my parents have knowledge of all the social media apps that I have accounts with?

Playtime

- Do I complain about the lack of playtime?

- Has my playtime ever affected my studies?

- Have I refused to let go of my playtime during exams and test days in school?

Music addiction

- Do I listen to bad music?

- Am I addicted to music?

- Do I have the habit of listening to music while studying or doing my homework?

- Do I listen to music that is not suitable for my age?

- Do I listen to songs without my parents' knowledge and consent?

Soft drink addiction

- Do I consume more than the usual amount of soft drinks?

- Do I always prefer sugary drinks?

Friendships

- Do my parents know all of my friends?

- Do I stay away from friends who engage in bad language?

- Do I stay away from bad company, who engage in sinful activities?

- Do I spend too much time talking/ chatting with my friends?

Bullying

- Have I been compassionate to weaker kids?

- Do I form groups in school or when I play and leave out certain people?

- Am I kind to kids who are new to my school or neighborhood?

- Did I cyberbully anybody (to bully a person through electronic means such as texts, emails, or social media apps)?

- Did I post any private pictures or videos of others without their permission?

- Have I made fun of children and called them names?

- Do I join groups or be with kids who are mean to other kids?

Respect for my body

- Do I eat healthy foods?

- Do I eat on time?

- Do I take my medicines without complaining?

- Do I give enough rest and sleep to my body?

- Do I spend too much time with my gadgets, thereby harming my eyes (vision) and overall health in general?

- Do I pay attention to personal hygiene (regular shower, grooming, etc.)?

- Do I play in a way that might cause injury to myself or others (rough play)?

- Am I too lazy to take care of myself? (Brushing teeth well, etc.)?

- Do I exercise regularly (walking, physical play)?

- Do I listen to very loud music, thereby damaging my hearing?

- Do I put myself in undue danger by my actions (misusing electricity, etc.)?

- Am I careful and cautious when I am walking or playing where there is ongoing traffic?

- Do I run in public places such as school corridors, thereby putting undue danger upon myself?

- Do I wear clean clothes everyday?

- Am I always sitting in one place and playing with my gadget?

Love of neighbor

- Am I kind and gentle with other children?

- Have I been unkind or rude to others?

- Do I pray for all my friends?

- Do I help people in need?

- Do I pray for the kids who are mean to me or people who hurt me?

- Have I held any grudges against others?

- Have I not forgiven anybody?

- Do I hate anybody?

- Have I treated other children with respect?

- Am I kind and gentle with children who are younger than me?

- Am I kind and welcoming to all guests who come to my home?

Discrimination

- Do I exclude others from play or activities because they are of a different race or color?

- Am I mean to others who are different from myself?

- Have I made fun of people's race or color?

- Have I made fun of people's accents or how they talk?

Unhealthy Competition

- Do I have a positive attitude when I compete with others in games and studies?

- Do I get upset and dejected if I lose in a game or someone gets better grades than me?

Cruelty to Animals

- Do I treat my pet with love and care?

- Have I ill-treated my pet or other animals in any way (pulling the tail, etc.)?

The Sixth Commandment

You shall not commit adultery

For Boys

- Do I show respect for girls?

- Do I give privacy and space for my sister and other girls?

- Do I knock on my sister's door before I enter?

- Do I knock on my parents' door before I enter?

- Did I tease or make fun of girls?

- Am I rough with girls?

- Do I look intently at people who are not dressed properly?

- Do I cover my private parts when I am in front of others?

- Do I deliberately touch or play with my private parts?

For Girls

- Do I show respect for boys?

- Do I respect my brother's privacy and give him space?

- Do I knock on my brother's room before I enter?

- Do I knock on my parents' door before I enter?

- Did I tease or make fun of boys?

- Do I deliberately touch or play with my private parts?

The Seventh Commandment

You shall not steal

Food

- Do I waste food?

- Do I take more than what I can eat?

- Am I stubborn about eating junk food all the time?

- Do I refuse to eat if the food that is given to me does not appeal to me?

- Am I a picky eater?

- Do I always want to eat out?

- Do I refuse to eat my food?

- Do I complain when I am given leftover food?

Clothes

- Do I complain about the lack of clothes?

- Do I wear clothes that are considered indecent (too revealing)?

- Do I take good care of my clothes?

- Do I demand expensive brand name clothes?

- Am I unhappy if I am given handed down clothes of my older sibling?

Toys

- Do I always demand for more and more toys?

- Do I take good care of the toys I own?

- Do I donate my toys after I use them or hand it down to my younger sibling?

Gadgets

- Do I always feel the need to upgrade to the newest phone or gadget?

- Do I always want to have the most expensive brand of phone or gadget?

- Am I saving money, only to get a new gadget?

Wastage of Energy

- Do I turn off the lights in my room upon exiting?

- Do I spend too much time watching television or other powered devices, thereby wasting electricity?

- Do I keep gadgets running when I am not using them?

- Do I waste water or consume more than the normal amount while showering, etc.?

Essentials

- Do I waste stationery (pens, pencils, crayons, and paper)?

- Do I waste my parents' money by buying or asking for unnecessary things?

- Do I cause minimal damage to the things I use and hand it down to my sibling or donate it?

Time

- Do I waste my time doing nothing?

- Do I waste my time doing unproductive things (watching shows, browsing the internet, or playing video games)?

Generosity

- Have I been kind and generous with my friends?

- Do I help people at home and outside (community service, donating, etc.)?

Cheating

- Have I cheated or been unfair in games and competitions?

- Have I ever cheated on tests or exams?

- Have I used a calculator or other devices to do my work without permission?

Stealing

- Do I return things in the condition I borrow?

- Have I shoplifted?

- Did I borrow something without permission?

- Have I stolen anything from the school library or from friends?

- Did I deliberately damage (scribbling, ripping pages, etc.) any books or media that I borrowed from school or friends?

Plagiarizing (Copying)

- Have I ever cheated by copying others' homework and claimed it as mine?

- Have I copied anything from the internet and claimed it as my own work?

Piracy

- Have I downloaded any content from the web without my parents' knowledge?

- Did I purchase or order anything over the internet without my parent's permission and knowledge?

Vandalizing (Destroying Property)

- Have I deliberately destroyed any object/appliance at home?

- Do I draw/scribble on the wall and cause damage to the house?

- Have I drawn/scribbled on the wall in school or other public places?

Holiday Gifts

- Do I demand too many gifts during Christmas, birthdays, and other special occasions?

- Do I get sad if I do not receive any gifts?

- Do I look for and demand expensive gifts or brand name gifts?

- Do I get jealous if my sibling gets more gifts than me?

- Do I get sad if I do not get what I expected?

- Do I see Christmas and other Christian holidays as a time solely to give and receive gifts?

Use of Money

- Do I use gift money responsibly?

- Do I waste pocket money that is given to me?

The Eighth Commandment

You shall not bear false witness against your neighbor

Lying

- Have I lied to my parents in general?

- Have I covered up (hide) any sin or wrong - doing?

- Have I lied to my teachers?

- Have I lied to my parents about my grades?

- Have I told lies to protect myself or escape from punishment?

- Did I blame others for my mistake?

- Do I come up with false excuses when I don't do my homework?

Bad Language

- Have I used bad language?

- Have I used unkind words?

- Have I cursed?

- Do I use any curse words that I heard from movies/ television or learnt from others?

- Have I used words that my parents or other elders have told me not to use?

Rumors

- Do I tattletale (telltale)?

- Do I complain about others?

- Do I share secrets that aren't supposed to be shared?

- Did I share bad things or false information about others over social media?

- Did I share information, videos, pictures of people without their permission?

Gossip

- Have I spoken bad things about people?

- Did I listen to gossip with interest?

- Do I talk about people behind their backs?

Teasing

- Have I teased anyone?

- Have I teased or made fun of any celebrity by sharing about them online?

- Have I teased or made fun of any religious person?

- Did I hurt or wound people's feelings by calling them names?

Honesty

- Am I honest in everything I say and do?

- Am I faithful in everything I do?

Boasting

- Do I boast about my abilities or qualities?

- Do I boast about my family's wealth (things we own)?

- Do I boast about my accomplishments, such as grades and awards?

- Do I boast about my toys and gadgets?

- Do I boast about the brand name things that I own?

Courtesy and Manners

- Am I courteous to others?

- Am I thankful for all the favors that I receive from people?

- Do I say "thank you" for all the favors received?

- Am I understanding and considerate toward elderly people?

- Am I kind and gentle with other kids?

- Do I use "please" and "excuse me" when making a request or seeking a favor?

- Do I ask for forgiveness from people if I have done some wrong to them?

- Am I good (welcoming) to people who visit my home?

The Ninth Commandment

You shall not covet your neighbor's wife

Modesty

- Am I modest in my speech and not use bad (dirty) language?

- Do I treat my body and other people's bodies with purity and respect?

- Have I watched television shows, movies, or pictures that are bad?

- Do I watch shows or movies that are not suitable for my age?

- Do I use any bathroom words (potty words) in my speech?

- Do I wear clothes that show too much of my body?

- Do I pray to the Holy Spirit when I am weak and tempted?

The Tenth Commandment

You shall not covet your neighbor's goods

Stealing

- Have I stolen money or other valuables from home?

- Do I carry any banned substance (phone) with me to school?

- Have I stolen toys or other items of interest from school, stores, or from friends?

- Have I stolen anything from my friends?

Envy and Jealousy

- Am I envious or jealous of the things or abilities that others have?

- Am I jealous when others get better grades than me?

- Am I jealous when others get an award?

- Am I jealous when others get appreciation or praise?

- Have I prayed for anything evil on people I don't like?

- Am I jealous of my siblings if they get more attention from my parents?

- Do I envy kids who are rich?

- Have I ever wished that other kids should fail the test or get bad grades?

- Have I ever wished that kids who I don't like should get into some kind of trouble?

- Am I jealous of kids who are popular in school?

A Quick Examination before going for confession

- Have I deliberately not prayed because of sleepiness or tiredness or have I been moody and rebellious about prayer?

- Do I read the Bible daily?

- Have I given more importance to anything (toys, gadgets, friends, fun, sportspersons, superheroes, movie stars or pop stars),) other than God?

- Have I read any occult novels or literature (Harry Potter, Twilight Series, etc.) and do I have any occult novels or books at home?

- Have I used Ouija boards or tarot cards as a toy?

- Have I watched any occult (evil) television shows or movies?

- Do I believe in lucky numbers, lucky colors, or objects to bring me good luck?

- Do I believe in superheroes, fairies, and other unreal creatures?

- Have I lied in the confessional?

- Did I ever forget to do the penance given by the priest?

- Have I hidden any sins in confession (insincere confession)?

- Did I confess without being truly sorry for my sins?

- Have I used God's name carelessly or irreverently (without respect) or in any casual joke?

- Did I use God's name in anger or did I ever get angry at God? ?

- Have I cursed using God's name?

- Have I laughed or shown interest when somebody shared a joke that spoke about God in a bad way?

- Did I continue to watch a movie that spoke about God in the wrong way or did I read or have books that speak about God in a bad way?

- Did I complain about anything (money, parents, lack of freedom, lack of toys, weaknesses, studies, homework, etc.)?

- Did I show disrespect in Church (failing to genuflect, not blessing myself with holy water, disturbing my parents, talking, playing with toys, playing with my gadget, etc.)?

- Have I played with or used any holy object (Rosary, scapulars, Holy Bible, blessed images) as a toy?

- Have I made fun of any priest, nun, or other religious persons?

- Did I make any promises and not keep them?

- Did I use God's name when making promises to others?

- Did I spend Sundays solely on fun and entertainment?

- Did I deliberately miss Mass on Sunday?

- Did I show disrespect during Mass (disturbing my parents, talking, playing with toys, playing with my gadget, etc.)?

- Did I miss Mass on any holy day of obligation?

- Did I fail to recite the Way of the Cross during Lent with my family or by myself?

- Did I grieve my parents by my words or actions?

- Have I shown anger (raise my voice) or hatred toward my parents?

- Did I disobey my parents?

- Did I bring dishonor to my parents?

- Did I demand for things or have I spoken in a demanding way with my parents and elders?

- Have I ever taken sides when my parents fought or did I cause any fight between them?

- Did I ever fight with my parents and not talk to them?

- Have I made fun of my parents or mock them?

- Have I spoken against my parents to others?

- Have I ever been ashamed or embarrassed of my parents?

- Did I act unkindly toward my siblings and fail to love them?

- Did I watch anything on television or the internet without my parent's knowledge and permission?

- Have I misused the internet access that was given to me for things other than educational purposes and games approved by my parents?

- Have I hidden any bad grades that I scored or done something bad at school?

- Do I have any sinful habit or addiction that my parents are not aware of?

- Do I ignore my parents when I am told to do my chores?

- Have I gotten angry at anybody, or did I hit anyone?

- Have I destroyed any personal property, things at home, or school property, as a result of my anger and temper?

- Did I play or download video games or apps without my parents' permission?

- Did I stay up late using my gadget, without my parents' knowledge?

- Did I talk to any strangers (adults) in chatrooms or social media apps?

- Did I listen to bad or unchristian music?

- Did I cyberbully anybody (to bully a person through electronic means such as texts, emails, or social media apps)?

- Did I post any private pictures or videos of others without their permission?

- Did I make fun of anybody or called them names?

- Did I join groups or be with kids who are mean to other kids?

- Have I been unkind or rude to others?

- Did I exclude others from play or activities because they are of a different race or color?

- Did I make fun of people's race,color, accent, or how they talk?

- Have I ill-treated any animal (pulling the tail, etc.)?

- Did I waste food?

- Did I wear clothes that are considered indecent (too revealing)?

- Am I addicted to my gadget (phone, tablet, gaming console)

- Have I cheated or been unfair in games and competitions?

- Have I cheated on tests or exams?

- Have I used a calculator or other devices to do my work without permission?

- Have I shoplifted?

- Have I stolen anything from the school, school library, or from friends?

- Did I deliberately damage (scribbling, ripping pages, etc.) any books or media that I borrowed from school or friends?

- Have I ever cheated by copying others' homework and claimed it as mine?

- Have I copied anything from the internet and claimed it as my own work?

- Did I purchase or order anything over the internet without my parents' permission and knowledge?

- Did I deliberately destroy any object or appliance at home?

- Have I lied?

- Did I blame others for my mistake?

- Have I used bad language?

- Have I used unkind words?

- Have I cursed?

- Did I tattletale (telltale)?

- Have I spoken evil about people?

- Did I boast?

- Did I carry any banned substance (phone) with me to school?

- Have I prayed for or wished anything evil on people I don't like?

- Have I been envious or jealous of anybody?

Scriptural Rosary for Children

Praying the Rosary added with scriptures serves two purposes. Firstly, it makes us seek the prayers of our Blessed Mother, and secondly, it helps us memorize Bible verses. In the Rosary given below, verses are carefully picked that speak about the commandments, confession, and sins that will help us examine our conscience and prepare for a good confession. It is a good practice to recite this Rosary before going for the weekly confession.

Make the Sign of the Cross.

I Believe…

Our Father…

Hail Mary…(3 times)

Glory Be…

Decade 1
Our Father…

If we confess our sins, he is faithful and just, to forgive us our sins, and to cleanse us from all iniquity. (1 Jn 1:9, DRA)
Hail Mary…

Do not be ashamed to confess your sins. (Sir 4:26, NRSVCE)
Hail Mary…

Have you sinned, my child? Do so no more, but ask forgiveness for your past sins. (Sir 21:1, NRSVCE)
Hail Mary…

One who is wise is cautious in everything; when sin is all around, one guards against wrongdoing. (Sir 18:27, NRSVCE)
Hail Mary…

If you love me, keep my commandments. (Jn 14:15, DRA)
Hail Mary…

My children, listen to me: happy are those who keep my ways. Hear instruction and be wise, and do not neglect it. (Pro 8:32-33, NRSVCE)
Hail Mary…

My child, do not forget my teaching, but let your heart keep my commandments; for length of days and years of life and abundant welfare they will give you. (Pro 3:1-2, NRSVCE)
Hail Mary…

We receive from him whatever we ask, because we obey his commandments and do what pleases him. (1 Jn 3:22, NRSVCE)
Hail Mary…

The love of God is this, that we obey his commandments. And his commandments are not burdensome. (1 Jn 5:3, NRSVCE)
Hail Mary…

You shall love the Lord your God with all your heart, and with all your soul, and with all your mind. This is the greatest and first commandment. (Matt 22:37-38, NRSVCE)
Hail Mary...

Glory Be...

Decade 2

Our Father...

If you worship me, the Lord your God, I will bless you with food and water and take away all your sicknesses. (Exo 23:25, GNT)
Hail Mary...

Those who fear the Lord do not disobey his words, and those who love him keep his ways. Those who fear the Lord seek to please him, and those who love him are filled with his law. (Sir 2:15-16, NRSVCE)
Hail Mary...

You shalt not swear falsely by my name, nor profane the name of your God. I am the Lord. (Lev 19:12, DRA)
Hail Mary...

My beloved, do not swear, either by heaven or by earth or by any other oath, but let your "Yes" be yes and your "No" be no, so that you may not fall under condemnation. (Jas 5:12, NRSVCE)
Hail Mary...

In six days the Lord made heaven and earth, and the sea, and all things that are in them, and rested on the seventh day: therefore the Lord blessed the seventh day, and sanctified it. (Exo 20:11, DRA)
Hail Mary…

Children, obey your parents in the Lord, for this is right. Honor your father and mother—this is the first commandment with a promise: so that it may be well with you and you may live long on the earth. (Eph 6:1-3, NRSVCE)
Hail Mary…

Children, obey your parents in everything, for this is your acceptable duty in the Lord. (Col 3:20, NRSVCE)
Hail Mary…

The Lord honors a father above his children, and he confirms a mother's right over her children. (Sir 3:2, NRSVCE)
Hail Mary…

Those who honor their father atone for sins, and those who respect their mother are like those who lay up treasure. (Sir 3:3-4, NRSVCE)
Hail Mary…

Those who respect their father will have long life, and those who honor their mother obey the Lord. (Sir 3:6, NRSVCE)
Hail Mary…

Glory Be…

Decade 3

Our Father…

Honor your father by word and deed, that his blessing may come upon you. (Sir 3:8, NRSVCE)
Hail Mary…

Do not glorify yourself by dishonoring your father, for your father's dishonor is no glory to you. (Sir 3:10, NRSVCE)
Hail Mary…

The glory of one's father is one's own glory, and it is a disgrace for children not to respect their mother. (Sir 3:11, NRSVCE)
Hail Mary…

My child, help your father in his old age, and do not grieve him as long as he lives; even if his mind fails, be patient with him; because you have all your faculties do not despise him. (Sir 3:12-13, NRSVCE)
Hail Mary…

Hear, my child, your father's instruction, and do not reject your mother's teaching; for they are a fair garland for your head, and pendants for your neck. (Pro 1:8-9, NRSVCE)
Hail Mary…

Love your neighbor as yourself. (Matt 22:39, NLT)
Hail Mary…

Be kind one to another; merciful, forgiving one another, even as God has forgiven you in Christ. (Eph 4:32, DRA)

Hail Mary…

I give you a new commandment, that you love one another. Just as I have loved you, you also should love one another. By this everyone will know that you are my disciples, if you have love for one another. (Jn 13:34-35, NRSVCE)

Hail Mary…

Bear with one another and, if anyone has a complaint against another, forgive each other; just as the Lord has forgiven you, so you also must forgive. (Col 3:13, NRSVCE)

Hail Mary…

Forgive your neighbor the wrong he has done, and then your sins will be pardoned when you pray. (Sir 28:2, NRSVCE)

Hail Mary…

Glory be…

Decade 4

Our Father…

Let all that you do be done in love. (1 Cor 16:14, NRSVCE)

Hail Mary…

The commandments say, "You must not commit adultery. You must not murder. You must not steal. You must not covet." These—and other such commandments—are summed up in this one commandment: "Love your neighbor as yourself." (Rom 13:9, NLT)

Hail Mary…

Whether you eat or drink, or whatsoever else you do, do all to the glory of God. (1 Cor 10:31, <small>DRA</small>)
Hail Mary…

Do not lie to one another, seeing that you have stripped off the old self with its practices and have clothed yourselves with the new self. (Col 3:9-10, <small>NRSVCE</small>)
Hail Mary…

Whatever you do, in word or deed, do everything in the name of the Lord Jesus, giving thanks to God the Father through him. (Col 3:17, <small>NRSVCE</small>)
Hail Mary…

Whatever you do, work at it with all your heart, as though you were working for the Lord and not for people. (Col 3:23, <small>GNT</small>)
Hail Mary…

Do you not know that your body is a temple of the Holy Spirit within you, which you have from God, and that you are not your own? For you were bought with a price; therefore glorify God in your body. (1 Cor 6:19-20, <small>NRSVCE</small>)
Hail Mary…

Your eye is the lamp of your body. If your eye is healthy, your whole body is full of light; but if it is not healthy, your body is full of darkness. (Luk 11:34, <small>NRSVCE</small>)
Hail Mary…

Do not love the world or the things in the world. The love of the Father is not in those who love the world. (1 Jn 2:15, NRSVCE)
Hail Mary…

How can young people keep their way pure? By guarding it according to your word. (Ps 91:9, NRSVCE)
Hail Mary…

Glory be…

Decade 5

Our Father…

You shall not steal. You shall not lie, neither shall any man deceive his neighbor. (Lev 19:11, DRA)
Hail Mary…

Let no evil talk come out of your mouths, but only what is useful for building up, as there is need, so that your words may give grace to those who hear. (Eph 4:29, NRSVCE)
Hail Mary…

Do not judge others, so that God will not judge you, for God will judge you in the same way you judge others, and he will apply to you the same rules you apply to others. (Matt 7:1-2, GNT)
Hail Mary…

Let your light shine before others, so that they may see your good works and give glory to your Father in heaven. (Luk 5:16, NRSVCE)

Hail Mary…

My children, our love should not be just words and talk; it must be true love, which shows itself in action. (1 Jn 3:18, GNT)
Hail Mary…

Which of you desires life, and covets many days to enjoy good? Keep your tongue from evil, and your lips from speaking deceit. (Ps 34:12-13, NRSVCE)
Hail Mary…

Entirely out of place is obscene, silly, and vulgar talk; but instead, let there be thanksgiving. (Eph 5:4, NRSVCE)
Hail Mary…

Do not devise a lie against your brother, or do the same to a friend. Refuse to utter any lie, for it is a habit that results in no good. (Sir 7:12-13, NRSVCE)
Hail Mary…

Do not be fooled. "Bad companions ruin good character." (1 Cor 15:33, GNT)
Hail Mary…

What do you have that you did not receive? And if you received it, why do you boast as if it were not a gift? (1 Cor 4:7, NRSVCE)
Hail Mary…

Glory Be…

Sacrament of Reconciliation

What are the basic steps of confession

- Examine your conscience

- Be sorry for your sins

- Decide not to commit that sin again

- Confess your sins to a priest

- Do the penance

What are the two commandments that Jesus gave?

- You shall love the Lord your God with all your heart, and with all your soul, and with all your mind

- You shall love your neighbor as yourself

What are the seven capital sins?

The seven capital sins are pride, anger, greed, envy, sloth, gluttony, and lust.

What are the precepts of the Catholic Church?

There are five precepts in the church, they are;

- You shall attend Holy Mass on Sundays and holy days of obligation

- You shall confess your sins at least once a year

- You shall humbly receive your Creator in Holy Communion at least during the Easter season

- You shall keep holy the holy days of obligation

- You shall observe the prescribed days of fasting and abstinence

Why should we confess our sins to a priest?

Because Jesus said so. The below verse is taken from the Gospel of St. John, where Jesus is giving this command to the apostles to hear confessions and to forgive (absolve) the sins of the people.

He breathed on them and said to them, "Receive the Holy Spirit. If you forgive the sins of any, they are forgiven them; if you retain the sins of any, they are retained. (Jn 20:22-23)

What is Repentance?

Repentance is the act of acknowledging our sins and feeling sorry for it.

What is the Act of Contrition?

The Act of contrition is a prayer by which we tell God that we are sorry for our sins, and we will never repeat it and avoid everything that leads us to sin.

What is Penance?

It is an exercise for our spiritual good. Penance can be a prayer, namely, the Our Father, the Hail Mary, or any prayer that the priest may recommend. Some priests will ask us to read a chapter of the Psalms or other books in the Bible. Others may instruct us to spend some quiet time in front of the Blessed Sacrament.

What is mortal sin?

Mortal sins are sins whose object is grave in matter and which is also committed with full knowledge and free will (full consent)

What is venial sin?

Venial sins are sins that are not serious. It does not affect our friendship with God. Little venial sins we commit slowly push us to commit a mortal sin.

What are sins of omission?

Sins of omission are committed when we have a duty to do something, but don't do it.

What is reparation?

Restitution (reparation) is to give back what we have stolen or taken without permission. On occasions when we cannot give back what we have taken, we should offer prayers for those who have suffered losses because of us.

How to Confess

- Begin your confession with the Sign of the Cross (In the name of the Father, and the Son, and the Holy Spirit, Amen)

- Bless me, Father, for I have sinned. My last confession was_____ (days/weeks/months/years) ago

- List out your sins. Confess all the sins and how many times you committed them

- Conclude by saying, "I am sorry for these sins and the sins I fail to remember."

- Wait for the priest's advice. Listen carefully to what the priest has to say. Most priests will encourage you by drawing you out of your sin and taking you to the love and mercy of God. They may also suggest or give some practical advice to overcome certain sins

- The priest will ask you to recite the Act of Contrition. The prayer goes like this,

O my God, I am heartily sorry for having offended Thee, and I detest all my sins because of Thy just punishments, but most of all because they offend Thee, my God, who art all-good and deserving of all my love. I firmly resolve, with the help of Thy grace, to sin no more and to avoid the near occasions of sin.

- Some priests will ask you to recite this prayer along with the penance after the confession

- Followed by the Act of Contrition, the priest will give a prayer of penance

- The prayer of penance can be a prayer or a Bible chapter that the priest may ask you to read. You may also be told to spend some time in front of the Blessed Sacrament

- Finally, the priest will recite the prayer of absolution. At this time, you should listen carefully to the words of the priest. The prayer goes like this,

God, the Father of mercies,
through the death and the resurrection of his Son
has reconciled the world to himself
and sent the Holy Spirit among us
for the forgiveness of sins;
through the ministry of the Church
may God give you pardon and peace,
and I absolve you from your sins in the name of the Father,
and of the Son and of the Holy Spirit.

- When the priest permits you to leave, thank the priest and leave the confessional

- Find a quiet corner in the church. If the Blessed Sacrament is exposed, you may sit before the Lord or sit where the tabernacle is located

- Do the penance that the priest gave you. Also, be sorry for your sins and promise God that you will never repeat it

- Finally, thank God for forgiving your sins

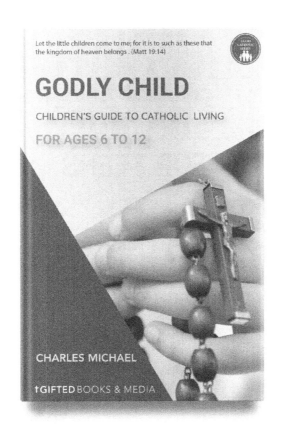

GODLY CHILD

CHILDREN'S GUIDE TO CATHOLIC LIVING

FOR AGES 6 TO 12

Now on Sale
Available in Paperback and Ebook
www.giftedbookstore.com

EXAMINATION OF CONSCIENCE
For Teens

Now on Sale
Available in Paperback and Ebook
www.giftedbookstore.com

EUCHARISTIC ADORATION

Prayers, Devotions, and Meditations

Includes Biblical Prayers and Scriptures to Meditate

This Book does not include Traditional Prayers

Now on Sale
Available in Paperback and Ebook
www.giftedbookstore.com

More Titles from Gifted Books and Media

RETURN TO GOD
Confession Handbook

PREACHER'S HANDBOOK

SCRIPTURAL ROSARY
1000 Bible Verses

GOD'S PROMISES AND BLESSINGS
FOR AN ABUNDANT LIFE

30 REASONS TO GO TO CONFESSION

EXAMINATION OF CONSCIENCE
For Teens

TO JESUS WITH MARY
*Scriptural Rosary on the Life and
Ministry of Jesus*

SCRIPTURAL STATIONS
OF THE CROSS

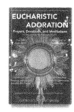

EUCHARISTIC ADORATION
*Prayers, Devotions, and
Meditations*

GODLY CHILD
*Children's Guide to
Catholic Living*

EXAMINATION OF CONSCIENCE
For Children

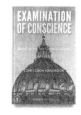

EXAMINATION OF CONSCIENCE
For Adults

Now on Sale
Available in Paperback and Ebook
www.giftedbookstore.com

Made in United States
Orlando, FL
24 July 2024

49488363R00055